Earn Money with Swagbucks
A Step-By-Step Guide to Passively Earning Money Using
Swagbucks and Kickfurther

Jeff Boyer

Γ

Gamma Mouse
www.gammamouse.com

Introduction

We would all like to "get rich fast", but other than starting your own business that skyrockets quickly—think Google or Facebook, among others—it isn't a very likely possibility. I equate it will hitting the lottery; it would be awesome if it happened, but I'm not holding my breath. I prefer real, actionable steps that one can do to actually make money. It might not be a lot of money, but learning to maximize even small amounts is incredibly valuable. So this guide will not peddle the "get rich quick" dream—I will leave that to other "gurus"—instead I will offer a great way to earn money easily, as well as a way to make that money work even harder for you once you've earned it.

My motto is "work smarter, not harder", and the suggestions detailed in this guide will take that idea to heart. With that in mind, this book is written to be brief and concise, quickly giving you the step-by-step knowledge you need so you can immediately do the most important step—take action! Don't expect to go through hundreds of pages looking for an outline of the necessary steps; you will get an overview immediately in the first chapter. This way you can take action quickly if you clearly understand the process. Less time spent reading is more time available to you to be making money! For those who want a more detailed explanation, subsequent chapters will cover the material in a more extensive manner. Whether you learn better with short explanations or longer, more detailed ones, this guide has you covered.

This process is less about tricks and more about using online websites available to you in order to make a little cash. It is basic—and may even seem self-evident to some—but the process is about making small amounts of money, and then maximizing it. This is not a model that will promote making money and spending it; the money we make might only add up to beer money per month, so spending it won't get you far. Instead, we will focus on taking these small amounts and making that money work for us—passively. Forget spending, we are going to use this money to invest. You may be asking: "Don't I need hundreds, or even thousands, of dollars to invest in something?" Not really. There are good opportunities available online in which you can invest only $20, an amount you can easily earn each month from Swagbucks. Don't worry if this doesn't make sense yet. I promise it will.

One final thing to mention before we get started. Years ago, a friend of mine—who was an incredibly successful internet marketing guru—gave me a copy of his notes that outlined his best strategies for making money online. This guide had been an invaluable marketing resource for me over the years, and I would like to offer it to you for free as a way to pay it forward. Before you start reading, I invite you to download your free copy at http://gammamouse.com/quit_your_job.

Method Overview

Before diving down into the nitty-gritty of this method, I wanted to give an overview of the process in a step-by-step format. If a step doesn't make complete sense here, don't worry—I will cover it in more detail in subsequent sections. On the other hand, if you understand how the process works from this outline, feel free to stop here and begin implementing these ideas. The sooner you get started, the sooner you will begin earning money. That should be enough of a disclaimer—let's get started!

1.) If you haven't already, sign up for an account at Swagbucks (swagbucks.com). For those unfamiliar with Swagbucks, it is a website in which you can complete various activities—like watching videos, answering surveys, and doing web searches—in exchange for points. These earned points can be redeemed for a variety of gift cards. This is how we will raise our seed money that we will invest.

2.) Start earning points on Swagbucks. I favor doing activities on Swagbucks that can be done passively. The best examples of this are watching videos-particularly through the Swagbucks mobile phone app or SBTV mobile phone app. Both of these apps will continuously play videos and earn points whether you are watching them or not. Often I will leave the app going at night while I'm sleeping; it's an easy way to collect a set amount of points each day without having to do anything. You can also have your desktop play videos, since this will also cycle through them to earn points. The task here is just start collecting points.

3.) Keep earning points until you hit 2500, then redeem these points for a $25 Paypal gift card. It will take a few days for Swagbucks to send your reward, so be patient.

4.) Sign up for an account at Kickfurther (kickfurther.com), which offers a new take on crowdfunding. Businesses use Kickfurther to raise money so that they can buy more product inventory. The users of the site crowdfund this new inventory, which essentially makes them owners. The company is then responsible for selling the product and paying back investors with an agreed upon interest rate. Rates vary by opportunity, but most of them fall within the 8%-12% range. There is risk, of course, but it is mitigated by the fact that the investors own the inventory that is produced. Therefore, if a company struggles to pay back its investors, the inventory can be liquidated in order to pay back investors.

5.) Add the Paypal funds you earned from Swagbucks to your Kickfurther account. Once your

Kickfurther account has been funded, it is time to browse some of the offerings on Kickfurther. If one appeals to you and you believe it a good investment, contribute your $25 to the cause. You will only be charged if the business meets their monetary goal, otherwise, your money will be returned to you. I generally look for companies that already have sales to invest in, since these are the safest bets.

6.) Keep earning points at Swagbucks, and go through the process again when you hit 2500 points. Grab the Paypal gift card, transfer the money from Paypal to Kickfurther, and invest in a new business opportunity with the funds. Since you will only be investing small amounts ($25) with different companies each time, this is a great way to diversify and lower your overall risk.

7.) As companies pay you back, always reinvest the funds once you have hit the minimum contribution limit (which is $20). We want our money to constantly be working for us!

By following these seven steps, you will be surprised at how just earning small amounts on Swagbucks here and there and investing that money on Kickfurther can lead to hundreds of dollars in a year. Not bad—considering all the work can essentially be done while you sleep.

Well, this wraps up the step-by-step overview of the method. If you are confident that you have a grasp on it, I suggest getting started immediately. The quicker you can start investing in inventories on Kickfurther, the more money you will make. For those who want a more detailed description of each step, let's move on to the first step.

A Closer Look

If you aren't a member of Swagbucks yet, the first step is to sign up for an account at http://www.swagbucks.com. If you are unfamiliar with Swagbucks, the site allows you to earn points while doing various activities. You can earn points for watching videos, searching the web, filling out surveys, answering questions, playing games, or signing up for a variety of services. The one thing you want to be aware of is that some offers require you to sign up with your information or even spend money to complete and get the points. Usually, these types of activities have high point totals for their rewards. We want to avoid these as the point of this method is to make easy money without spending a dime. Because of this, we are going to focus exclusively on watching videos for our points. I encourage you to search the site and see what is available to do for points; many of them just require more work and effort than I wish to do for this method. The point is to make this process as passive as possible.

Tools that are extremely helpful for watching videos on Swagbucks are the free mobile phone apps, which should be available at your favorite app store. Swagbucks is the more general app; it has other activities than just watching videos on your phone. The SBTV app is dedicated to only watching videos. Both apps allow you to pick the first video, and then it will automatically cycle through to subsequent videos, earning you points along the way. There is a daily cap to how many points you can earn through these apps, so you will want to take advantage of that.

You can also watch additional videos on Swagbucks when you access it directly through the website. Once again, you can start a video and it will cycle onto additional videos until you earn your points reward. I usually have no problem earning 100 points a day passively just using these two methods, and it requires little effort from me. While 100 points per day is not going to make you rich, you have to remember that this process is a marathon and not a race. You can always do more activities on Swagbucks to earn points at a faster rate in order to hit your ultimate goals, but it isn't necessary. However, some people find some of the other activities fun and enjoy doing them and have the time, so I don't want to dissuade you from that if that is you. Just don't spend money on activities in order to earn points; it isn't worth it.

Now that we know about Swagbucks and how we are going to earn points—and eventually gift cards—from them, let us turn our attention to how many points we need to ultimately earn, and how we should spend those points in purchasing our reward.

What to Do with the Points You Earn

Now that you have started to bank points in Swagbucks, it is time to talk about our endgame here. We want to earn enough points to purchase a $25

Paypal gift card, since we can use our Paypal account to fund our Kickfurther investments. There are a ton of choices in the Swagbucks Rewards Store, from physical items to gift cards. The gift cards come in multiple denominations, and start for as little as $3 (or 300 points in your Swagbucks account). The smallest value Paypal card you can purchase is for $25, which will require you to have at least 2500 points in your Swagbucks account.

Once you hit the 2500 point milestone on Swagbucks, go to the Rewards store, search for gift cards, and search for $25 denomination. Once you have found the Paypal card, you will have to click on "Snag It" to place your order. You will have to verify your order, which can be done easily through an email that Swagbucks will send you almost immediately after you place the order. Verify it, and then sit back and wait for your reward gift card to be delivered. Swagbucks states that it can take around 10 to 14 business days to receive your gift card, so be patient until then. Personally, I don't think I have ever had to wait that long for a gift card; most of the time, I seem to get it in a week. In the meantime, you want to continue earning points on Swagbucks—there is your next 2500 points and $25 Paypal gift card to think of. So keep earning while you wait for Swagbucks to fill your reward.

Once Swagbucks has fulfilled your reward, and made your Paypal account $25 richer, it is time to make that money work for us. We will do this by investing with one of the most unique crowdfunding websites out there—Kickfurther!

Using Kickfurther

Now comes the point where we need to sign up with Kickfurther, a crowdfunding website that lets you invest your money in a company's inventory in exchange for a flat rate of return. This rate of return varies with each offer but can be anywhere from 4% to 20% over the course of 3 to 10 months. Kickfurther is also expanding rapidly, and has been offering more and better opportunities as they become more established. You can sign up for an account at kickfurther.com.

I recommend that after you sign up, you take a moment to browse both current offers and previous funded offers; this will give you an idea of some of the innovative companies and products you can invest in. Also, now would be a great time to fund your Kickfurther account; you can easily do that through your Paypal account, transferring the $25 we earned from Swagbucks. I also encourage you to sign up for email alerts, which will allow Kickfurther to email you when a new offer has been posted. Some of the latest opportunities have been reaching their funding goal in minutes, so email alerts gives you a chance to contribute before the offer is funded. This is especially important since the better offers tend to hit their funding goals quickly.

It is important to understand how Kickfurther works. This is not a loan that you are giving to the company, rather you are purchasing a stake in their inventory which they will then sell. As the business sells their inventory, they will make payments to Kickfurther which are then distributed to the contributors who funded the project. The inventory in this situation serves as collateral, which Kickfurther has the ability to liquidate if the company fails to pay back their obligations in a timely manner. This helps to manage the risk involved. Also, companies are limited with how much money they can ask for initially. Once they have run a successful campaign, and paid back their backers, they can run another offer with a much higher limit. This means that most first-time business offers on Kickfurther are seeking about $10,000, which is great for not letting these companies get in way over their head.

Here are a couple of things I look at when deciding whether to contribute to an offer. Make certain that the company is actually making sales; most will post some recent revenue figures. You also want to know where they will be selling the product. In my mind, the more sales channels the better.

I always approach offers thinking about the audience and market for a product. Who can I imagine buying the product? Do I think this is a large audience, or a small one? There are some really interesting and innovative products on Kickfurther, but that doesn't necessarily mean I think they have a huge market waiting for them. Many of the offers on Kickfurther originally ran successful Kickstarter campaigns. This means they have developed and fulfilled at least one round to their Kickstarter backers. But this doesn't mean they have sales channels or a larger market to sell additional product. My point is that the best way to exercise caution and not lose money—even the small amounts you are investing—is to look at the company and products honestly. There are a ton of cool and innovative products that never sell, because they lack marketing and an audience. So develop your instincts and intuition to spot these before contributing your hard-earned cash.

Once you have found an offer that interests you, contribute your $25, and then sit back and enjoy your money working for you. Kickfurther has a timeline on each offer page which will tell you when payments are expected, so you can keep track of company's sales progress.

You have done it! You earned $25 through Swagbucks, and have now invested it in a Kickfurther project that can bring you back a nice rate of return over a short period of time. But we aren't finished yet! Now we can go back to Swagbucks and start the process over again, banking points by watching videos until we have 2500 points again for an another Paypal gift card. That's more money you can fund your Kickfurther account with, and use to invest to another business offer. The more money you have to invest in different offers, the more you will earn in return. So get started and take action!

Also, when companies begin paying you back, you will have money in your Kickfurther account that you can re-invest (once it clears the $20 minimum contribution limit). By re-investing, we can continue to have our money passively earning interest. How great is that?

While this method won't make you rich, it can make you a nice little savings fund. Think about it—if you started in January and continuously earned Swagbucks through the year, invested that money in Kickfurther offers, and re-investing your returns, you could have a sizable Christmas fund for gifts by the end of the year. How awesome would that be? Especially since it is so easy to do!

Taking Action is Key!

I encourage you to take action today, and get started earning Swagbucks. The sooner you start the more you can earn! I hope that this modest method helps you earn some extra money. As prices rise and budgets get stretched, I know that every little bit you can earn helps. I will consider this guide a huge success if my readers are able to put this process in action, and earn an amount of money that impacts their lives. I truly hope that you were helped by this!

WAIT! Before You Leave…

Download the #1 Bestseller from Gamma Mouse Media for FREE! Hurry this offer won't last as it is for a limited time only. Reserve your free copy today at http://gammamouse.com.

A Special Gift for Our Readers!

Thank you so much for your purchase of this book. As a special gift for you we have included one of our bestselling Self-Improvement books: Procrastination: Triple Your Productivity and Accomplish Your Goals written by one of the most well-respected and influential experts on time management, Warren R. Sullivan.

I hope you enjoy!

Procrastination
Triple Your Productivity and Accomplish Your Goals

Warren R. Sullivan

Gamma Mouse
www.gammamouse.com

Introduction

Procrastination. It has a drastic effect on productivity, on our ability to accomplish our goals in life. It can greatly impact our happiness, as we avoid doing something that we are dreading. Yet having to do it still hangs over our head.

Delaying something in order to often do something easier is an easy trap to fall into. Do it enough, and it suddenly becomes a habit. The problem with procrastination is we usually put off more important—but also more difficult—objectives for doing actions that are more trivial. For example, a college student might watch television rather than write a report.

Our time is valuable. It is the one thing that cannot be replaced, unlike money or objects. Yet it is wasted when we procrastinate. Saving this time should be our goal. We need to realize that our time would be better spend on accomplishing our most important objectives. When you have finished those, then reward yourself.

Stopping our procrastination is as easy as changing our attitude and stopping the habit that we have fallen into. In reading this guide, you will learn the tips and tricks necessary to stop procrastinating and start living. You don't have to suffer any longer, you can be happy and more productive, accomplishing all the important goals in your life quickly and easily. But you must take the first step and make a commitment to change yourself. Reading this book is a start, but if you don't act on what you learn change will not come. So consider this a call to action, a chance to truly change your life.

Getting to the root of the problem

Everyone procrastinates. It is part of being human. Whether because of laziness or not having the energy to tackle a difficult task, we choose to relax, to take the easy way out. Understand that not all procrastination should be viewed as bad. Often we need a break from the rigors of our day, a chance to get away from the stress of life. Some goals require great effort and energy to complete, so tackling them when you don't have much energy is realistic.

The line we don't want to cross is when we fool ourselves into believing that laziness is not having the energy to complete our task. Our first step is to recognize when we are being lazy. Clearly, we need to be honest with ourselves, we need to hold ourselves accountable. Secondly, we need to realize that time is our most valuable resource, and that it is finite. No one knows how much time they have, so it is essential to understand how important time is. When you sit down to watch television, recognize that this is time you will never get back.

To borrow a phrase from economics, understand that there is an opportunity cost to ever action you take. When you choose to do something, you lose the opportunity to use that time differently. When you make a choice, there is always a cost, remind yourself of this when you find yourself procrastinating. One of my methods for reminding myself to utilize every minute of my time as effectively as I can is to write the number 1440 on the white board in my office. This is the number of minutes in one day. Whenever I find myself procrastinating, I look at my board, and it helps me refocus on my task at hand.

People procrastinate for different reasons. The first step is to understand the reasoning behind our procrastinating. There may be more than one, but understanding the psychology behind our choices will help us effectively combat them, allowing us to change our faulty reasoning when it arises.

Cognitive distortions are a form of irrational thinking that often lead to procrastination. It is a magically type of thinking. Often we believe that we will be better equipped at some point in the future to handle our task, rather than completely the task at that time.

An example is a person who believes that they need to be in a certain mood in order to complete a task successfully. Or a person may believe that their motivation will increase in the future, and thus will be in a better position to accomplish their goals. Another one that happens in business quite frequently is an employee overestimating the time they have left to complete a task while also underestimating how long it will take them to do it.

If you are putting off a task, because you believe that you will be better suited in the future, realize that you are committing a fallacy. There is no evidence suggesting that your belief is true.

When we are confused about how to complete a task, and the details involved, we may procrastinate giving the reason that we need further instructions before we can continue. This allows us to set the project aside, until we find that we are butting up against a deadline. This reasoning often comes up with perfectionists who do not want to start a task until they are confident in their ability to complete it perfectly. To combat this reasoning, understand that completely the task initially to the best of your abilities and understanding, and then waiting for feedback is much more productive. It is easy to make corrections to your mistakes once the task is completed, as opposed to trying to do the task perfectly the first time. And there is always the possibility that the goal will be accomplished on your first attempt, without the need for further clarification. Don't fool yourself into thinking that if you have additional information, you will be better suited to complete the task. This is a cognitive distortion.

An offshoot of this is avoiding a task because you don't know how it should be done, that you require procedural information. Once again, this reasoning arises most often in the perfectionist, who believes they need to wait for the perfect situation in order to be successful. But look at the great inventors throughout history, who only through trial and error found out how to accomplish something amazing. Imagine if they had waited for the perfect moment, these inventions may never have come into existence. Remember that your goal is to accomplish your task, mistakes that you make can always be corrected. Don't fear failure. Instead, recognize it as an opportunity to learn.

I used to suffer from thinking I needed to take the time, to contemplate and reflect, before beginning a job. What I was doing was procrastinating, convincing myself I needed more information. This was clearly a logical fallacy. Thinking about the job was not going to make me more productive. What was going to make me more productive was doing it. If you believe you need more time to accomplish something, stop and examine whether that is true. Even if it is true, you can start the task now and revise it later as your thoughts begin to coalesce.

We have all had tasks that we had to do that we really didn't want to do. Income taxes come to mind. It is a responsibility, and sometimes that additional pressure makes a task unpleasant. And we are human, we do not want to do things we find unpleasant. We may even fool ourselves into thinking that there will be a point in the future when it will be easier to deal with an unpleasant task. Never make the mistake to think that a task that is unpleasant today will somehow miraculously improve in the future. It is always better to get the unpleasantness over immediately, rather than wait. I am reminded of my public speaking class in college. I always wanted to go first, and I could never understand why people wouldn't want to be first. Most found public speaking uncomfortable and unpleasant, but instead of immediately getting it out of the way and then relaxing, they chose to prolong how long the task would take them. Don't fall victim to this. If you find a task unpleasant, do it immediately; procrastination only makes it worse, and in the process makes you unhappy.

Now the opposite of procrastinating over tasks that we find unpleasant is to procrastinate over accomplishing goals that we don't care about. Finding the effort to complete a task when you are indifferent to the outcome is difficult. Often we may believe that we will feel more inclined to complete a task in the future when we feel more connected with the outcome. Usually indifference does not change, people don't suddenly start to care. These types of tasks often don't get tackled until we run up against a deadline. This can cause us additional stress as we must now take time to complete a task we don't care about instead of tasks that are much more important to us. Understand the cost of procrastinating may not be felt until the future when the task must be completed. Completing the task immediately saves you from future repercussions that you cannot anticipate.

I previously relayed the example of people believing that at some point in the future they will be in a better mood to accomplish a task. They may believe that certain moods make them more productive and believe that they need to wait for when they are in that mood. Recognize that this is an irrational reason you are giving yourself in order to procrastinate. While your emotions can affect your work, this is only generally in the case of extremes. Slight fluctuations in mood will have no effect, so don't convince yourself that you will be in a better mood to complete the task in the future. There is no truth to this.

A more specific example of this idea that a certain mood is essential for higher productivity is the case of individuals who wait until the last moment to start a task. The student who begins to study for mid-terms the night before the text, or the employee who starts an project the day before it is due are two examples of this. Waiting until the last minute to start because you think you are more productive up against a deadline is nothing more than believing that your mood makes you more productive at a point in the future. Don't fall for this procrastination excuse.

An additional reason you don't want to wait until you are up against a deadline is the cognitive distortion in which you overestimate the time you have while underestimating how long it will take you to accomplish a task. If you wait, believing you work better under pressure, you may place yourself in a situation in which you have significantly underestimated the time you will need. This may cause you to rush, resulting in sub-standard work. Or, even worse, you may miss your deadline completely. Avoid backing yourself into this corner where time works against you. Remember that we often believe that we have more time than we actually do.

Another reason people often give for procrastinating is that they had forgotten about a job. Often the reason that it was forgotten is intentional, the task may be unpleasant or one that we are indifferent about. If a deadline is far into the future, it can be easy to forget about our upcoming responsibilities. Or we may believe that we will get to it closer to the deadline. Understand that this is procrastination, and that there is nothing keeping you from completing the job now.

The final cognition distortion I will address is the belief that you don't want to currently complete a job because you are not feeling well, and that you will wait until you feel better. It should be evident how this is very similar to waiting for a specific mood in order to complete a task. Understand that there is no guarantee that you will feel better, in fact, you may end up feeling worse. Granted that people suffer from real health problems that greatly impact their ability to be productive. This is not what I am referring to. Instead, I refer to procrastinators who exaggerate how they feel to shirk their responsibilities. Don't be disingenuous with yourself about how you feel in order to avoid doing something.

Many of these cognition distortions are rooted in perfectionism or in our fear. We are either waiting for the moment to be right, or we are waiting to overcome our fear to do a task we may find unpleasant. Tell yourself that the moment will never be perfect, but it will be good enough to get the job done. Or if you are dealing with fear, realize that confronting your fear and doing the job now, will mean that once you have finished you will no longer have anything to fear. In fact, you will likely feel elated. This is a much better situation to be in than living under a cloud of dread.

Now that we have explored the underlying psychological reasons behind procrastination, our attention will turn to effective methods for dealing with procrastination. By employing the appropriate methods to our life, we will be able to become happier and more productive people.

Recognize the problem

Like with any addiction or problem, the first step is always to recognize and accept that you have a problem. Since you have purchased this book, I will assume that you have identified yourself as a procrastinator, and are now taking the proper steps to remedy this.

Do not feel shamed or embarrassed, identifying and attacking your problems is a noble and brave action. Focus on your self-awareness; stopping procrastination means keeping a keen eye on your behaviors. And making the necessary corrections.

Exercise

I want you to exam your behavior and thought processes. Write down three incidents in which you procrastinated.

Refer to the previous chapter if you want to show why your reasoning was faulty.

Find the root of the problem

Why are you procrastinating? Are you a perfectionist? Is fear keeping you from accomplishing certain tasks? Be honest with yourself. Discovering the root of your procrastination is important. If you recognize the cognition distortions that you are employing, this will give you a hint at the root of your procrastination. While knowing the underlying cause is helpful, identifying your faulty reasoning so you can correct it will have greater long-term gains.

If you are a perfectionist or if fear is holding you back, I want you to take a moment and examine your thinking. Why do you have to be perfect? Does it make you more productive? Does it make you happier? My guess is the answer will be "no". Tell yourself that accomplishing something perfectly is not the goal, the goal is only accomplishing your task. Withhold judgment, jobs are either done or not done. Also, ask yourself is it true that the longer you wait, the closer you will be to perfect? Or would you have done the same job either way? Does the evidence actually support your way of thinking?

The same approach can be taken if you suffer from fear. Ask yourself what you are afraid of? Most people fear a specific outcome. Is it rational to believe that outcome is guaranteed? I may fear dying in a plane crash, so I dread getting on a plane. But what are the chances that this event actually occurs. My chances are much greater of dying in a car accident on the way to the airport, but I don't have the same dread getting into a car. By nature, fear is not rational; it often arises from the fact that we have convinced ourselves of a terrible outcome, even though that outcome may be incredibly remote. Try to look at your fear rationally; assess the likelihood of the outcomes you fear. Then ask yourself: is it really that bad? Surprisingly, our fears are often overstated; they have a tendency to shrink when we look at them rationally.

Exercise

Using the previous chapter, identify any cognitive distortions you have fallen victim to. Can you discern what is behind this? If it is fear or the desire to be perfect, look at potential outcomes. Does it really need to be perfect? Is it a situation that you should be fearful of? Write down the reasons why you believe you need to be perfect, or write down why you should be afraid. Put it away for a day, and then read it again. Do your thoughts appear logical?

Prioritize with lists

Writing down a list is very effective in helping you achieve your goals. But you need to stick with it. Many people write lists, and then don't follow them. Remember the list is to help you stop procrastinating. Once you write the list, don't convince yourself out of following the order you set.

Put the jobs in order of priority, the most important being first and the least important being last. Estimate how long you believe each task will take you. Then multiply that time by a factor of three. Set this revised time as your deadline. The extra time will take into account the possibility that you are underestimating how long each task will take you; it serves as a buffer. The benefit is that if you complete your tasks early, you now have that extra time to do things you want to.

Keep your list close at hand. You can either write it down, or like I do, keep it on a mobile device.

There are numerous to-do list apps that will simplify the process.

Exercise

Write a list in which you prioritize your tasks by level of importance. Decide how long it will take you to do each task, then multiply that number by three. Write down the time needed next to each task on your list.

Divide and conquer

There are some tasks that are so large and unwieldy that estimating how long they will take is an incredibly difficult job. To help facilitate the process, break the large job into smaller segments. These segments should be small enough that you can estimate the time each one of them will take. Make certain you add in a buffer by multiplying each estimated time by three.

If you have a specific deadline, you can now add the time estimations for each of the smaller tasks to arrive at a figure for the entire project. This is a fantastic way to estimate large projects without placing yourself in a stressful situation as the deadline approaches. In fact, this approach is used quite frequently in the software industry for large multi-team projects.

Exercise

If you have a large project on your list, particularly if you are having difficulty estimating how long it will take, break it down into smaller segments. Now evaluate how much time each task will take, keeping the added buffer in mind.

Keep distractions to a minimum

One of the biggest productivity killers in recent years for businesses has been the Internet. It becomes easier for employees to procrastinate when they have other options that are more appealing only a mouse click away. With social media and email, there is always something new happening, and it can be quite difficult not to get immersed in this flow of constant information.

There are productivity plugins that will limit your access to the Internet by allowing you to stay online for short periods of time. If possible, I also recommend shutting down your email program, and only checking it at designated times. One method that is effective is to focus on your task for the first 50 minutes in the hour. In the remaining ten minutes, you can then check your email or Facebook status.

Additionally, a work or home environment can be distracting. People talking, a television playing, and other background noise can make you lose your focus. Listening to music through headphones or using earplugs is effective in blocking out distracting noise.

Exercise

Are you being distracted? Analyze your environment and decide whether you are being distracted. If you find yourself going online to check email or surf the Internet, try to use the 50 minute rule. Browser plugins will also limit your access to the Internet. Research, install, and configure them if you need this level of restriction.

If noise is a problem, buy earplugs or bring your headphones and MP3 player in order to listen to music.

Celebrate your accomplishments

You have completed your task list; time to celebrate. Giving yourself a reward after accomplishing your goals is wonderful way to encourage yourself to leave procrastination behind. The reward can be anything, an hour of television, a movie and dinner out, or an item you want. The point is to make it something you really desire, to properly give you a sense of accomplishment.

Exercise

Schedule a reward for yourself for completing your task list. Make it good. You deserve it.

Take care of yourself

Eating right and sleeping the recommended amount by your physician is essential in helping to reduce stress and anxiety. It is much easier to tackle your task list if you are feeling energized after a good night's sleep followed by a substantial breakfast. Often poor eating habits during the day lead to your blood sugar crashing in the afternoon, leaving you feeling sluggish and tired.

Make a point of eating a balanced diet spread over at least three meals over the course of the day. Maintain a regimented sleeping schedule. Try to go to bed and wake up at approximately the same time every day. Maintaining our sleep rhythms is very important.

Exercise, put it as a high priority on your task list if you have to. This can be as simple as taking a short walk. Exercising has the wonderful effect of increasing your energy, so take advantage.

Exercise

Evaluate your eating and sleeping habits, making the necessary changes. If you are not exercising, start. It can be as simple as a thirty minute walk per day.

Learn to say no

Many of us have the tendency to want to please other people. We take on more tasks and responsibilities than we have time for, causing us to have too many things to accomplish and not enough time to do them in. If you become too overwhelmed, there is a very good chance you will procrastinate rather than tackle your enormous list.

Learning to say no to task of low importance is key. When someone asks you to do something, look at what they are asking objectively. Is this task a high priority to you? What is the opportunity cost to you? Remember that your time is extremely valuable, it cannot be replaced. Time you spend on this task could be spent elsewhere. Unless it is a close family member, the most time I'm willing to spend on a task for someone is ten minutes. If I don't think I can accomplish it in ten minutes (after adding in my buffer), I will apologize and tell the person that I can't do it. Most people understand, they realize that we all lead busy lives. And if they don't, it is only further justification that I made the right decision.

Exercise

Look at your task list. Are there low priority jobs on it that you agreed to do for other people? If so, remove them from your list and let the person know, unless you believe you can accomplish it in a very short timeframe.

Be proactive in obtaining the information you need

During our examination of cognition distortions, we talked about procrastinating because we lack specific information about how to proceed or what our ultimate goal was. The way to avoid this problem is to always ask questions immediately on being given the task. Make certain you understand what your deliverables will be as well as the best way to proceed. There is no harm in asking and getting the answer. It will save you both time and aggravation.

With the advent of cellphones and email, people are generally accessible within a few hours. If the person you need to ask is not available, try to ask someone who has completed a similar task. Asking questions is not only an effective method for curtailing procrastination, it also has a generally positive affect on your life. We live in a society where the majority of people ask too few questions.

Exercise

Examine your task list. Is there a task that you have questions about? If so, contact the person who can answer your questions immediately. Even if it is late, send them an email. Don't wait, act on your questions right now.

Get into the habit

Procrastination is a bad habit, emphasis on habit. Habits need to be broken, and the best way to accomplish this is by replacing them with a new habit. If you have taken the suggested action to this point, you have already started on your way to replacing your habit to procrastinate. But it is only the start. Generally, it is believed that if a person can change their behavior for twenty-one days that change will become permanent.

Exercise

Find a calendar and mark off twenty-one days from today. Your goal is to keep up on doing your task list daily for the twenty-one days. Be aware that you will have to fight to keep procrastination from coming back in. Replacing old habits can be difficult, which means you need to remain vigilant of any back-sliding.

Make tasks relevant to you

Many of the jobs we do are done despite us being indifferent to the task or not enjoying it. The easiest way to combat this is to look at the task and accentuate a positive aspect of it. If you can find a good reason for doing something, it will make accomplishing it much more attractive to you. Think outside the box for reasons if you have to. Maybe completing a task will open up a new opportunity in your life, or allow you to connect with different people. Accomplishing it may give you the opportunity to make new friends.

There are a variety of reasons why a task should be completed. You need to find the one that holds the most appeal to you.

Exercise

Take a moment to examine your list. Are there any jobs you do not enjoy to do? Are there any tasks you feel indifferent about? If so, think of a good reason, one that appeals to you, of what completing the task could mean for you. Try to find a reason that makes you want to tackle the job.

Conclusion

I hope that you have found this journey helpful. If you have participated in the recommended exercises along the way, you should be commended. You have clearly decided you want to change, and that is a huge first step to becoming a more productive person.

Procrastination is not something you need to suffer with, the answers are all right here in this guide. Understand that procrastination can have deep psychological roots, causes that take time and effort to overcome. The best way to accomplish this is to face it head on. If you are a perfectionist, try completing a task even though you may not feel it is perfect, or up to your usual standards. If fear is holding you back, stand up to it by imagining the worst outcome, and then honestly evaluating how likely that outcome will come to be.

Humans suffer from many irrational thoughts, convinced of the truth of an idea even though the evidence suggests the opposite. Recognizing these irrational thoughts is the first step in dispelling them. Once you realize you are being illogical, the thought fails to hold any power over you anymore. Never take anything for granted, continuously question your thoughts, assessing them for validity. This isn't only the key to stopping procrastination, it also leads to a life that is happier and more productive.

I wish you all the success in your journey.

WAIT! Before You Leave…

Download the #1 Bestseller from Gamma Mouse Media for FREE! Hurry this offer won't last as it is for a limited time only. Reserve your free copy today at http://gammamouse.com.

www.ingramcontent.com/pod-product-compliance
Lightning Source LLC
Chambersburg PA
CBHW070950180526
45168CB00003B/1191